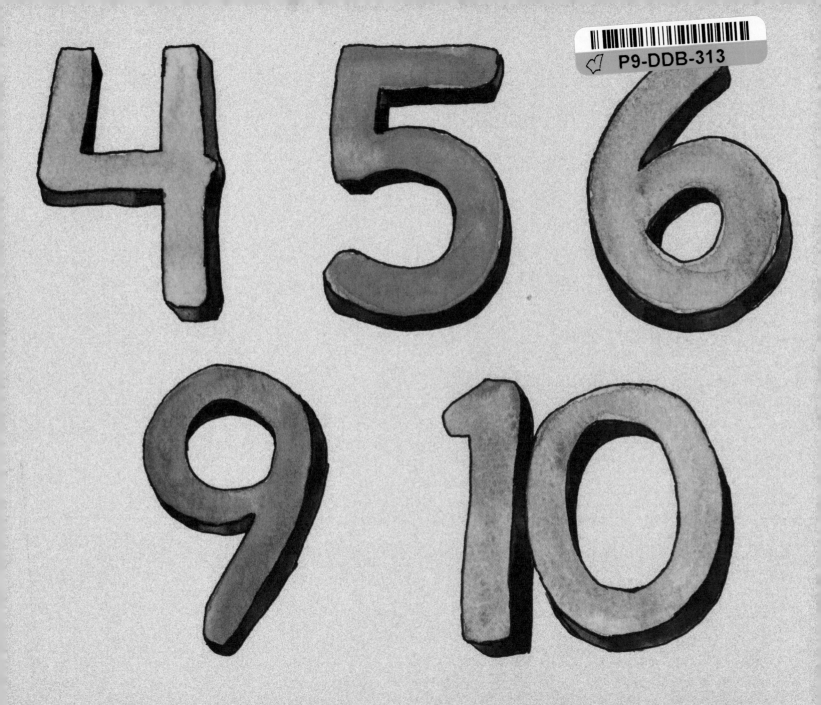

Published by Scholastic Inc.,
90 Old Sherman Turnpike, Danbury, Connecticut 06816.

SCHOLASTIC and associated logos are trademarks
and/or registered trademarks of Scholastic Inc.

ISBN 0-7172-8615-0

Printed in the U.S.A.

First Scholastic Printing, August 2005

My eight Book

by Jane Belk Moncure
illustrated by Paige Keiser

SCHOLASTIC INC.

New York   Toronto   London   Auckland   Sydney
Mexico City   New Delhi   Hong Kong   Buenos Aires

This is Little  .

Little  lives in the house of eight.

It has eight rooms. Count them.

Every day, Little  goes for a walk. One day, she walks to a farm. She sees

a mama hen.

Then she sees seven little
yellow baby chickens . . .

pop out from under the mama's wings.
How many are in the whole family?

Little eight opens a gate. She sees two brown goats,

two black goats,

and four white
goats in a pen.

Count the goats.

Little  opens the gate very wide.
How many goats run outside?

How many goats stay in the pen?

Just then the farm dog runs by. He chases . . .

two goats

back into the pen.

Little  counts the goats.

How many goats are missing?

Then two more goats run
back through the gate.

Does Little  count eight goats?

Little  hops to a grapevine. "I will pick a bunch with eight grapes," she says.

Which bunch does she pick?

Next Little  eight skips into the garden.

She picks two tomatoes,

two cucumbers,

two carrots,

 one head of lettuce,

and one radish  .

 How many vegetables does she pick all together?

"I will make a salad," she says.

Little  makes a very big salad.
She invites her bunny
friends to a picnic.

How many bunnies come?

"Let's play hide-and-seek," says one bunny.

Little  closes her eyes.
She counts to eight
very fast. Can you?

Away hop the bunnies.

Little  eight finds five bunnies

behind some bushes.

How many bunnies are still hiding?

Then Little eight finds three bunnies in a field of daisies. Has Little found all the bunnies?

23

"What pretty daisies," says Little  eight .
"I will give each bunny a daisy."

Little eight picks a bunch of daisies.

How many does Little eight still need?

The happy bunnies hop eight hops. Can you?

Little eight hops back home.

When Little  gets home, she invites her best friend to a tea party.

Little  and her friend each have a piece of cake.

How many pieces are left for you?

Little 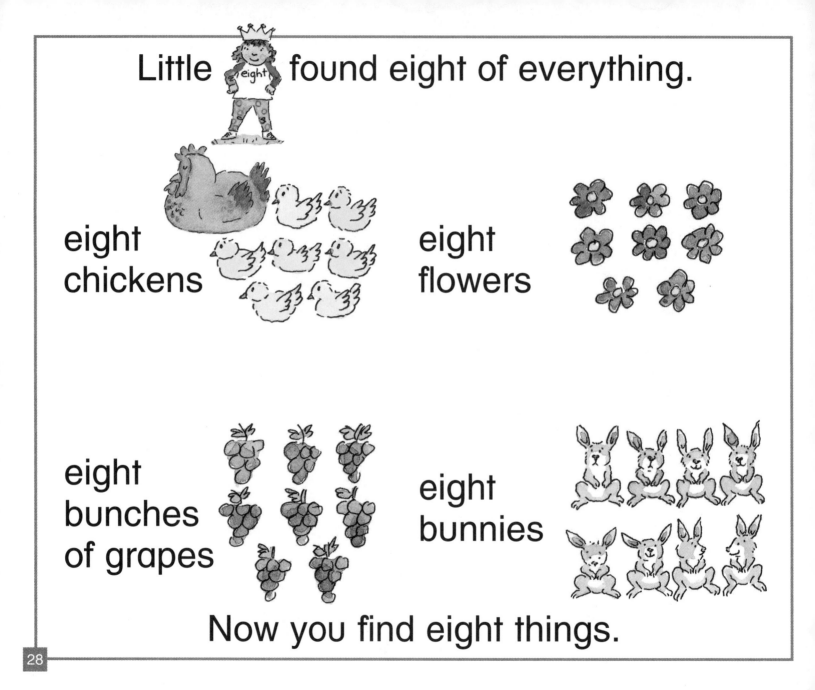 found eight of everything.

eight chickens

eight flowers

eight bunches of grapes

eight bunnies

Now you find eight things.

Little 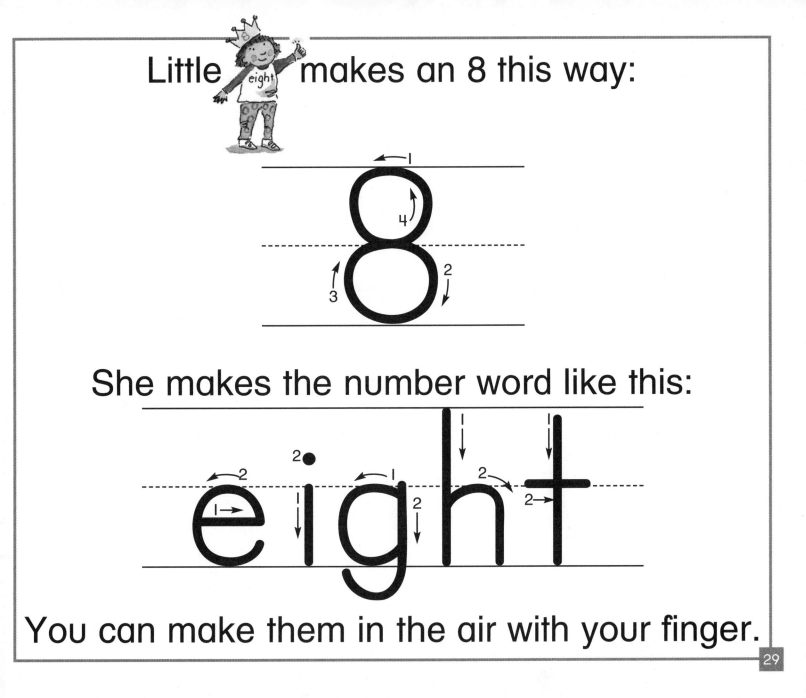 makes an 8 this way:

She makes the number word like this:

You can make them in the air with your finger.